Melissa,

I hope you love this book.

♡

Widowed 2

Now I Live

John Polo

better
not bitter widower

Widowed 2
Now I Live

By John Polo of Better Not Bitter Widower

Copyright © 2019 by John Polo

ISBN: 9781070651132

All rights reserved. No part of this publication may be reproduced, distributed, or transmitted in any form or by any means, including photocopying, recording, or other electronic or mechanical methods, without the prior written permission of the publisher, except in the case of brief quotations embodied in critical reviews and certain other noncommercial used permitted by copyright law.

www.betternotbitterwidower.com

Parchment paper on pages 41, 78, 79, 107 designed by nuchylee / Freepik

Pg. 36 - (couch) Designed by brgfx / Freepik, (man) Designed by rawpixel.com / Freepik

Pg. 60 - Designed by macrovector / Freepik

Pg. 63 - Photo by Jhonis Martins from Pexels

Pg. 85 - Designed by topntp26 / Freepik

Pg. 95 - <a href="https://www.freepik.com/free-photos-vectors/cute">Cute photo created by asier-romero - www.freepik.com</a>

Pg. 117 - Designed by Freepik

Pg. 195 - Image by <a href="https://pixabay.com/users/daniel64-231942/?utm_source=link-attribution&utm_medium=referral&utm_campaign=image&utm_content=735823">daniel64</a> from <a href="https://pixabay.com/?utm_source=link-attribution&utm_medium=referral&utm_campaign=image&utm_content=735823">Pixabay</a>

The Ripple Effect

I have something to say.

It. Is. Not. Just. The. Loss.

So many look at the loss as just a loss.

"Well, he lost his wife."

"Well, she lost her husband."

"Well, they lost their child."

I suppose, sometimes, that may be the case.

The loss is just a loss.

Far too often, though, that is NOT TRUE.

The ripple effect.

Society DOES NOT see the ripple effect that the loss has on one's life.

Society does not see the mom of four whose husband took his own life after a lifelong battle with mental illness, and how she and her children are now on the verge of being homeless.

Society does not see the dad who lost his wife to cancer and is now raising three grieving children on his own.

Society does not see the ache of Mother's Day, the desperation of Father's Day, and the never-ending void that hangs over each holiday season.

Society does not see the mom who worries that her children will develop the same type of addiction that took her husband.

Society does not see the dad whose heart drops as he takes his daughter shopping for clothes, and all the other little girls have their mommies alongside them.

Society does not see the widow whose husband passed away right before they tried to have children. Her heart breaks every time she sees a young family with a small child.

Society does not see the bills that cannot be paid.

Or the PTSD that cannot be avoided.

Society does not see the hurt behind Muffins with Mom.

Or the pain behind Donuts with Dad.

Society does not see the friendships lost.

Or the profound loneliness that ensues.

Society does not get it.

There is a ripple effect that occurs after a truly profound loss.

A ripple effect that society does not see.

We do not just deal with the loss of our love.

We deal with a whole new world.

A whole new world that, far too often, is marked with extreme worry and stress.

A whole new world in which you are left alone to navigate issues that were not present before.

A whole new world.

On top of a broken heart.

Guys, I know.

Believe me.

I know.

I see your struggle.

I struggle, too.

The ripple effect Michelle's death has had on my life has been beyond words.

I see your struggle.

And I fuckin love you.

You can do this.

Just breathe.

What does "strength" mean to you?

People Think I Am Strong

People think I am strong.

I used to think they were wrong.

Even foolish.

They didn't see me during my weakest moments.

When she had to pick me up.

As she fought for her life.

They didn't see my deep despair.

They didn't see me on the floor, crying so hard that my insides hurt.

The tears so powerful and loud that I worried a neighbor might hear.

The people who tell me I am strong, they weren't the ones who had to grab me tight.

And tell me that everything would be okay.

As I sobbed openly.

And without the ability to stop.

People think I am strong.

I used to think they were wrong.

And then one day I realized something:

They are right.

It is during our weakest moments, in which our strength is truly defined.

If you have yet to read my first book, *Widowed. Rants, Raves and Randoms*, I strongly suggest you put this one down and read that one first.

There is a method to my madness.

#please #dont #mess #with #my #flow

It's Complicated

I have it heard it before.

From them.

And.

From you.

"Only those who had good marriages can truly know grief," the man said with confidence.

Don't worry. I corrected him.

With kindness.

Patience.

And, most importantly, knowledge.

"I don't feel like I can relate. Everyone else had a fairytale marriage. My marriage was not a fairytale."

I hear it so often.

From strangers.

From clients.

And, yes, from friends.

Widows and widowers who hide in the shadows.

Widows and widowers who read the blogs, the books, and the Facebook posts.

Widowers and widowers who question their place.

Their place in our community.

Widows and widowers who question their love.

And their grief.

I know that there is a textbook definition for complicated grief.

Although, if I am being honest, I don't know what that textbook definition is.

Abuse. Betrayal. Infidelity. Suicide.

These, to me, represent complicated grief.

And complicated grief, to me, is a topic that needs to be discussed.

Respected.

And understood.

My wife died.

From a one-in-seven-billion cancer.

At the age of 30.

Diagnosed with the disease at the age of 27.

Just as we found our way back to each other.

After eight long years apart.

Just as we both found happiness.

After a lifetime of searching for it.

My story is not a fairytale; despite what some might think.

It is a tragic love story.

A tragic love story in which I lost the only woman I have ever loved.

A tragic love story in which my pain was so deep,
and my despair was so profound,
that I planned to join her.

Witnessing her die a slow death.

The images of her two-and-a-half-year cancer battle are seared into my memory bank.

For the rest of time.

The loss of the most amazing human I have ever known.

It broke my heart.

And it shattered my soul.

But as devastating as my loss was,
for as tragically beautiful as our love story might be –
my grief is somewhat simplistic.

I love my wife.

I miss my wife.

And I carry her love and memory with me every day, as I rebuild.

My grief, for as intense as it was and can still be, is not overly complicated.

I do not wake up at 8:00 a.m. with fear.

Fear that my spouse, who is now dead, may be in the other room.

Fear that today will bring another day of physical abuse.

For something that I "did wrong."

I do not have visions at noon.

Visions of the person who was supposed to be mine and only mine.

Stepping outside of our marriage.

And questioning myself as to why I was not good enough.

The rage and self-doubt so overwhelming that it feels as though you are choking on it.

I do not cry in the evening.

Because I miss my spouse.

And even with the abuse or infidelity that took place fresh in my mind,
I would do anything to have them back.

Even if only for a moment.

I do not breathe a sigh of relief moments later.

That they are gone.

And will never be able to hurt me again.

I do not get angry before bed.

For all the damage that their actions, behaviors and decisions did to me.

As the realization comes that, even though they are gone, the damage they did still impacts me today.

It impacts your mind.

Your heart.

Your body.

And your soul.

I do not sit, and stew, as I wonder what drove them to take their own life.

Going back and forth between blaming them and yourself.

Reliving every possible sign of their depression.

Questioning if, somehow, it was your fault.

I love my wife, so much.

I miss my wife, so much.

I mourn my wife, so much.

But, if grief from a healthy marriage has the ability to make us feel bipolar,
grief from a relationship that saw abuse, betrayal,
infidelity or suicide has the ability to make those left behind feel bipolar times 50,000.

Moments of fear and regret, followed swiftly by moments of relief.

Moments of love and remorse, taken over in an instant by feelings of intense anger.

I know some of you may be thinking, "Who is he to tell me this?"

You question my story.

You question how I, of all people, can speak to complicated grief.

I have seen it.

I have lived my entire life surrounded by abuse and infidelity.

I have lived my entire life surrounded by mental illness and suicide.

I have seen it in the faces of my friends.

And in the voices of my clients.

I have seen it in those that I have just met.

And in those that I have loved for years.

My message to all of those who had less than ideal marriages is this:

Your grief is every bit as valid mine.

Your pain is every bit as valid as those who had a good, or even great, marriage.

Your changing moods, thoughts, and emotions are not only acceptable, but are normal.

And to be expected.

You do not need to run from your truth.

You do not need to hide in the shadows.

You do not need to feel as though you do not belong.

So many share your story.

So many have a similar truth.

WHAT. HAPPENED. TO. YOU.

WAS. NOT. YOUR. FAULT.

We are not responsible for the actions and behaviors of other people.

Even when they are our loves.

Even when they are the one we chose to spend our life with.

YOU. ARE. NOT. RESPONSIBLE. FOR. THE. ACTIONS. AND. BEHAVIORS. OF. OTHER. PEOPLE.

Yes, what happened to you will stay with you for the rest of your days –
but, even so, there is a way to move forward.

There is way to move forward so that the pain walks alongside of you.

Instead of in front of you.

Honor your grief.

The anger. The fear. The sadness.

And the love.

Honor it.

All of it.

You are entitled to feel everything that you feel.

Do not run from your story.

You were a victim.

Now.

You are a survivor.

The humor I've added to this book may be even more deranged than the humor in my first book.

#brace #yo #self

And I'm sorry

We don't just miss the past.

We don't just miss the present.

We also miss the future.

We miss the future.

Missed.

Meet Cindy

Cindy met the love of her life, Steve, on a blind date.

"I met him on the Internet, before Internet dating was even a thing. It was 2004.

I decided to create a profile on Yahoo personals. I was with my family for Easter and I wanted to show my sister what I was up to, along with some of the creeps that were on there for a good laugh.

My sister started looking over my shoulder and then her boyfriend. By the time I knew it my entire family was interested in what I was doing.

One didn't like this guy, the other didn't like that guy.

But then we got to Steve.

They all agreed on Steve.

His eyes, they were so kind."

Cindy and Steve would meet, and as Cindy tells it, their first date was filled with laughter and non-stop conversation.

"We didn't even order for an hour because we were too engaged with each other to look at the menus."

The two would date, fall in love and become man and wife.

"We bought a house, got a dog, and started talking about having kids.

Our lives together were going to be beautiful."

In 2010, things began to change.

"Steve finally went to the doctor, and he was diagnosed with melanoma.

My mom had beat skin cancer, so after Steve's surgery, when the doctor told us that everything was removed and that there were clear margins, we figured that things would be okay.

We thought we had dodged a bullet."

That fall, the couple, who now had a new appreciation on life, found out that Cindy was pregnant.

"Evie came first, and then two years we would have Harper. We were now a family of four."

Everything was as they had dreamt it to be.

Until one day, when it wasn't anymore.

"I saw the look on Steve's face and I asked him what the doctor said," Cindy recalled.

"Metastatic Melanoma," he responded.

"What does that mean?"

"It's bad. It's really bad."

Steve, a man who had dedicated his life to being a husband, father and teacher,
now faced a diagnosis that threatened to put that life in jeopardy.

"We were still hopeful. Steve had a way of making everything better. Of making everyone laugh.

Even as we battled this horrible disease, it was because of him that all seemed okay."

As Cindy tells it, Steve loved nature, fantasy football, the environment, pizza,
rooting for the underdog, and playing sports with his daughters.

"He would get so excited when he would teach them about the planets," she recalled.

On February 4, 2017, Steve, the man who his wife called
'the most amazing human I have ever met', would pass away.

He was just two weeks' shy of turning 40 years old.

"After he passed away I crawled into bed with him. I got into "my spot" right under his arm,
put my head on his chest and strokayed his face. I knew this would be the last time
I would be able to do this so I wanted to burn it into my memory. The feeling of laying on his chest,
his smell, the feeling of his face, the shape of his fingers, kissing his face while it was still warm.
I couldn't leave. I didn't want to leave him. I laid with him for an hour."

Telling her girls that their father had passed, was a moment that Cindy will never forget.

"My daughter Evie asked if he was ever coming back. And I had to tell her no.
That moment will forever remain a dagger to my heart."

The man who had a knack for making his wife laugh, and easing her stress with his playful nature, and vibrant smile, had passed away far too early.

His legacy, though, that remains alive and well.

It lives on through his family, his friends and his students.

His wife.

And his daughters.

"I remember our last conversation. It was Saturday or Sunday. All the chemotherapy drugs made his throat really painful. Too painful to talk. I remember him sitting in the bed, looking at me and making the motion that he needed a drink.

I brought it to him and held both sides of his face.

"I love you honey."

He looked at me with sad eyes.

"I know you love me, too."

He looked at me with his big, kind eyes and nodded as to say "I do."

When I sat back down, he looked at me and blew me a kiss.

I blew him one back."

....

"I was so lucky to have married my best friend."

About 6 weeks after Michelle started chemo her hair started falling out.

Eventually it would not only be her head that was bare, but her entire body.

As we were driving to her work one day to stop in and visit, she discovered a single hair on one of her toes.

For the next six hours, until we got home, and she was able to pluck it off – I heard about this toe hair.

As did all of her friends and co-workers.

She showed it to them.

On the way home she sat there in the car and just stared at it.

"One toe hair John. My entire head is bald, I have no eyebrows, but I have one toe hair."

"Ok Michelle," I said, growing weary of the conversation by this point.

"Oh, I'm sorry John, but do you not find this fascinating?" she snipped back.

grief education #432

not dating doesn't mean you're stuck

just like dating doesn't mean you're over it

It must be easy.

For those who have never endured the horrors that this world has to offer.

To sit.

And cast judgement.

                                                                            It must be easy.

                                     For those who have skipped casually through life.

                                                     To cast judgement.

On those.

Who have walked.

                                                            Through the flames of Hell.

do not tell me how to:

1) love

2) grieve

3) heal

4) or live

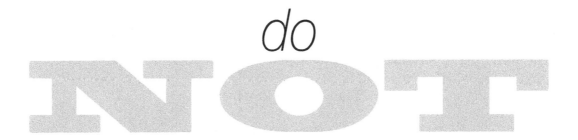

the way I grieve my spouse

is not subject to your fuckin analysis

Room 4

"What's your favorite number?" I asked Michelle, shortly after our reunion after eight long years apart.

"4," she responded with a grin.

"4? Why 4?" I asked, genuinely confused.

I figured it would be 11, or 22, or anything, really.

But why 4?

"In grade school, we were at the playground and everyone was saying their favorite numbers.
They asked me mine and I didn't have one.
I panicked, so I blurted out the number 4.
Now, I just say that whenever anyone asks me," she responded with a dorky chuckle
as she ate the last bite of her breakfast toast.

"You are such a dork, Michelle," I joked back.

"Yeah, but you love me."

I wanted to write something today.

Something powerful.

And heartfelt.

I wanted to write something moving.

And inspirational.

I wanted to write about our first New Year's Eve together in 2002.

The girl of my dreams by my side. We were so in love.

I wanted to write about our last New Year's Eve together.

December 31, 2015.

The day that we were transferred to hospice.

I wanted to write about the events leading up to that transfer.

I wanted to write about the feeling of pure fear and complete devastation we had as we left the hospital that day.

I wanted to write something about the gut-wrenching pain of a 30-year-old woman being taken to her final destination.

The place she would go to die.

I wanted to write about all of that.

I wanted to write about so much more.

I can't though.

Not today.

I have tried.

The words, they simply will not form.

So, instead, I want to tell you about Michelle's favorite number.

The number 4.

Terrified and heartbroken beyond anything that I can articulate with words, we left the hospital on that cold, snowy December day.

Upon arriving to hospice, they quickly checked us into our room.

"John. It's room 4," Michelle said as she gripped my hand tightly and attempted to hold back the tears.

"Yeah. It's room 4," I whispered back.

If You Had 5 More Minutes with Your Love, How Would You Spend It?

"I would smell him. I would tell him how much I miss him and that I still love him. Then, I would kiss him. I'd spend the rest of that time just kissing him." – Deanna

"I would yell at him. Yell at him for leaving me. I would yell at him for leaving me to live this life without him." – Sarah

"I would thank him. Over and over again. I would thank him for loving me the way that he did." – Ilise

"Naked and in the bed." – Megan

I would hold her.

I would hold her so tight.

And I would refuse to let go.

Not to sound like a jerk or anything, but I would LEGIT throw an organic cucumber at YOUR head if it meant that I could see Michelle again.

Even if only for a moment.

Allie

I was talking to a client the other day.

She is more than ten years out.

At the end of the call, she started to tell me how, sometimes, she feels like maybe she doesn't belong in the widowed community anymore.

She explained that, sometimes, she feels guilty around those that are so raw in their grief.

I told her that while her feelings were valid – that she was looking at it the wrong way.

I told her that those are the people who need her.

I told her that those are the people who she can truly make a difference for.

Those are the people who can look at her.

And they can say.

"She survived. So now I know that I can — *too*."

I Wish I Had You Way Back Then
(a message to the grieving community)

I wish I had you way back then.

When she was sick.

And I was watching her die.

I wish I knew you existed.

When I angrily cursed to a Higher Power.

And asked, "Why?"

I wish I had you way back then.

When I needed more than just a friend.

I could have used a word from someone who had been through it.

A helpful word. You could have sent.

I wish I had you way back then.

When the vision before me. I could take no more.

I wish I could have reached out to you.

You could have told me that I would survive. This unimaginable horror.

I wish I had you way back then.

As I sobbed so loudly. Yet, I made sure she could not hear.

I wish I had someone who had survived the same pain.

To sit with me. And share a tear.

I wish I had you way back then.

When I, myself. Wanted to die.

You could have told me what I tell others now.

Focus on survival. That is the first thing to do.

Learning to live again is possible.

"I promise, in time – it will happen for you."

I wish I had you way back then.

When making it to the next second. Seemed a task too great to bear.

To tell me in time that I would be okay. To acknowledge my belief, that none of this was fair.

I wish I had you way back then.

For the support you give me now.

I'm so thankful that I found you when I did.

Together, those of us who have made it through.

Must show the rest of the world how.

Last week I kindly posted on my Facebook page, requesting that someone come to my house ASAP, get the salad out of the fridge, put some dressing on it and bring it to me on my couch.

I was hungry and didn't want to move.

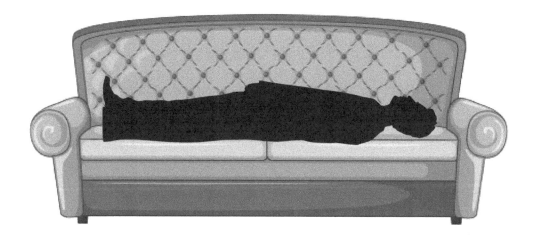

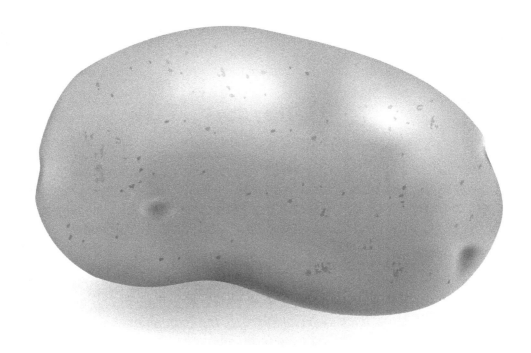

After sitting there for two hours, waiting for the doorbell to ring, I got up and made my own salad.

Honestly, I don't understand why all of my friends have to be SO fuckin lazy.

They Say

"When my oldest son asks for his daddy, I have to tell him that he won't be able to see him, but that he is always with us. He just looks at me and shakes his head 'no,' unable to understand the complexity of death at such a young age. The pain that I feel for myself is excruciating, but the pain that I feel for my children – it is simply unbearable." – Cassandra

"Having suffered from abandonment issues my entire life, after Michael passed away, those issues only grew worse. Unlike others who left me, it wasn't Michael's choice to go, but that didn't matter; the impact was just the same. It has been a long road, but through the process of learning to love myself, I am finding a sense of healing as I go." – Tatiana

"I don't think people realize how much we desire to talk about them. Personally, I crave people to say her name. I want people to mention Julie, to remember how wonderful she was and, yes, even to admit how awful it is that she is no longer with us. The ability to hear and speak of her feels like water, when I am dying of thirst." – Jay

"More than anything
I just want to feel okay again.

I just want to feel the way

I felt before my heart
became so pulverized,
one could snort it."

Shawna

January 6, 2014

Michelle is such a man that she never cries, so she just had an "emotional moment" but couldn't actually cry, so she faked wiping tears away when there were not any there and now she is giving me the finger as I call her out on it.

She was the best at love

Sneak Peek of My Upcoming Book
My Michelle

"Did you ever stop loving me, John?" she asked.

"No," I started.

"I could never stop loving you, Michelle."

The way we love someone.

Is unique.

So, why would the way that we grieve them.

Be any different?

I loved her my way.

I will grieve her.

My way.

Meet Jessica

Jessica met the first man she would ever love, Michael, in Spanish class.

He was 14.

She, one year younger.

"A mutual friend introduced the two of us and I just ignored him. I guess he didn't like that because he pulled a prank on me and I ended up slapping him across the face.

Believe it or not, from that point on, we were best friends."

One night as the two were driving, a song came on the radio.

"Back at One" by Brian McKnight.

As Jessica tells it, Michael pulled the car over and asked her to get out.

It was raining but, reluctantly, and with a little nudge from her best bud, she did.

"He turned up the radio and he made me dance in the middle of the street with him. In the rain. It was at that very moment that we fell in love."

The two dated for a number of years and married in 2003.

Michael and Jessica spent ten years together as man and wife.

They loved each other. And the life that they had built.

On February 6, 2013, after complications from a routine surgery,
Michael unexpectedly fell into a coma.

For the next eight days, Jessica laid by her husband's side.

And she refused to leave.

"On the day he died, I climbed into bed with him and I wrapped his arms around me.

And I placed my head on his chest."

On February 14, 2013, Michael took his last breath in the physical form.

"He died, but I felt like I did, too. We all did. He was our everything."

Before he got sick, Michael had made Jessica promise to take him to a concert.

"Although not wanting to, I ended up going to that concert.
And that is where I met Kyle.
I met him at the concert I was supposed to go to with Michael.
To this day, that very fact still floors me," Jessica recalled.

Nearly five years after the passing of her first love,
Kyle and Jessica became man and wife on December 26, 2017.

"It's so weird loving two people.
The way I love Michael, I am proud of being a wife again.
It is amazing to still feel that love for Michael and still be able to love another so deeply.

Michael wasn't my first chapter, and Kyle isn't my second chapter.

Each man is their own separate book.

I realized, on this journey, that my heart is capable of loving two.

I never would have thought it was possible.

But my heart is capable of loving two."

you thought I was going to put another bathroom selfie in this book.

didn't you?

y'all so cray cray

"Ever since Jeff died, I have been struggling with the concept of his legacy.

He had no children, didn't own a business or employ people,
never wrote a book or made a movie, never discovered or invented anything –
and yet, he was loved and respected by so many.

But what was his contribution?

How would he be remembered in the world, and by whom?

Then, I realized something:

I am his legacy.

The way that I live my life from here on out will be the way I remember him to the world.

For the love that he showed me and the life lessons that he taught me.

He was a man of such integrity, and he helped me to be the person that I am today."

Lisa

Anna

"My biggest regret is how impatient with him I was during his last ten months, especially when he was under hospice care.

I was in full-blown caregiver and advocate mode.

Looking back, I wish I had stopped this earlier and focused more on being his wife, and his best friend."

Meet Judy

Judy met the love of her life, Justin, in January of 2005.

"The day we met, we both had broken hearts, as each of our previous relationships had just ended hours earlier."

After attending the same party, the two found themselves cleaning up together around 4:00 a.m.

"He asked me out. I was so excited. To this day, I believe fate brought us together."

Sparks flew, but just three weeks after they met, Justin was in a serious car accident.

"He was in a medically-induced coma. The doctors did not think that he would make it."

Every week, Judy would send cards and letters to Justin's sister's house.

"On March 5th, I decided to call his sister to see how he was. He had just gotten out of rehab.

He was home, and he was okay.

He thanked me for everything that I had sent to him."

Three months later, the two would finally see each other again,
and that is when their whirlwind romance began to take off.

"We dated for a while and I would later find out that Justin's sister told him
she knew one day we would become man and wife.

It must have been the cards and the letters," Judy joked.

One day, as Judy was in the hospital herself, Justin decided to accelerate the relationship.

"He took me out to a park right behind the hospital, with my IV pole intact,
and he told me that he wanted a commitment. A month after that, he asked my
parents for their blessing and on October 2nd, 2005,
he took me on a horse and buggy ride in the middle of
Times Square and asked me to be his wife."

Justin and Judy would become man and wife thirteen months later.

"He was the most loving husband a girl could ever ask for.

We finally both had what we had always wanted.

True love. We were so happy.

It was perfect."

On July 27th, 2011, after complications from follow-up surgeries related to his car accident, Justin would fall into a coma.

"I sat there and I waited for him to wake up.
I hoped that he would open his beautiful, green eyes.

I hoped that he would see me again."

On September 2, with Justin in a coma, Judy asked the priest if he would renew the couple's vows.

The priest agreed.

"We became man and wife, again.

I didn't know if he would ever wake up.

I needed that moment."

Two days later, Judy would receive a phone call.

"I rushed to the hospital room. When I got there, I jumped into the bed with him.

I held him so close. I did not want to let go."

Justin had passed away just shy of their 5-year wedding anniversary.

His loving wife would honor him by giving his eulogy exactly six years to the day that he proposed.

"The truth is, I will always honor Justin as my eternal love. And I will always keep his memory alive.

I know that if I am ever meant for a new beginning, Justin will show me the way."

Hope is always there.

Even when it cannot be seen.

Felt.

Or identified.

Hold on.

Until you find your hope.

Never did I think I would smile again

For who can envision such a thing

When the thought of just breathing again

Seemed a task too great to bear

Never did I think I would breathe again

So many times I didn't want to

The thought of waking up in the morning without her

Talk about scare

Never did think I could survive the unimaginable pain

Of all that we endured

Never did I think I could walk this Earth

If my Michelle was not to be cured

Never did I think I would be sitting here

A man still so broken

Yet also, so repaired

Never did I think I would live again

I planned to take my own life

Through hope at the 25th hour

I was spared

I just used the pen that I am writing this book with to scratch my nipple.

I know you didn't ask.

But I thought about it for a while.

#and #i #really #thought #you #should #know

told ya

The truth is.

People only see what they want to see.

They don't see the tears that still come.

And the moments of missing them.

That still take your breath away.

They don't see the fight.

That you fought.

To survive first.

To exist second.

And to ~ eventually ~ live third.

They don't see the toll that the loss has taken on you.

On your mind.

Your heart.

Your soul.

And ~ yes ~ even your body.

They don't see.

How that loss still impacts you.

Each and every day.

They don't see.

What they don't want to see.

That even as we move forward.

The damage and pain of the loss.

Will never fully go away.

The void that is will be there in one form or another.

For the rest of our days.

They don't see.

The courage it took to hold on.

When you didn't think that you could hold on.

They don't see the will it took to exist.

When you may not have wanted to exist.

And they don't see the bravery in somehow actually living again.

When you never even thought.

That you could survive.

just because we remembered how to laugh

does not mean we forgot how to cry

we can be happy

and we can be sad

we can be both

at the exact same time

If you are a widowed person who struggles with self-esteem and/or self-worth, please know that you are not alone.

This is a huge issue in our community that does not get discussed nearly enough.

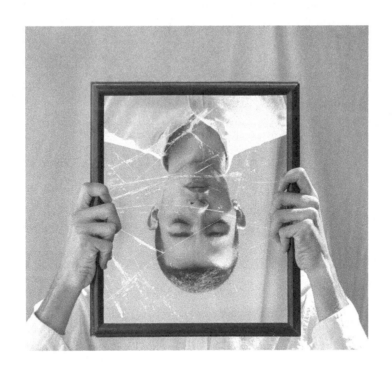

Meet Allison

"Austin and I met in the summer of 2010."

It was on their second date in which Austin told Allison that she had beautiful eyes, and that he couldn't wait for their kids to have them.

"On our third date, he told me that he loved me and that I would be his wife one day.

So, yeah, we moved a little quick, but he and I both just knew," Allison recalled.

Austin was right; Allison would be his wife one day.

A year after they met, the two exchanged their vows and would soon become parents.

"Everything was perfect. We had the life that I had always dreamed of."

Just over five years after their union, Allison would lose the man whom she loved.

"We lived in Texas and Austin was working in Philadelphia. I got the phone call that Austin had an aortic dissection. I had to make the decision to take him off of life support.

I flew to him and was able to say goodbye before he left us. My heart was shattered."

At the age of just 26, Allison found herself a widow with a 5-year-old son and twin 2-year-old girls.

To make matters even more tragic, Austin passed away on September 23, 2016 – the day that the couple's daughters would turn 2 years old.

"I didn't know how to be anything but a wife. The truth is, I don't remember much from the first eighteen months. I think I was just in shock, and going through the motions for my kids."

Allison describes Austin as her best friend, rock, soulmate, and protector.

"He was funny, generous, and kind. He was tough, but at the same time he was a big teddy bear."

As Allison found herself down a path of self-destruction, she knew something had to change.

"I ate and drank myself numb. I was up to 284 pounds. I was miserable and without an ounce of hope."

One day, Allison decided something needed to change, so she Googled "How to get over a dead husband."

"At first, I began to connect with other widowed people, and it helped me to know that I wasn't alone. After that, I began to work on my grief and life with John's help. Once I started to feel a sense that there might actually be hope on the horizon, the next step was to take charge of my physical health."

In one year, through diet, exercise, and the determination to live again, Allison has lost over 100 pounds.

"When Austin died, my self-esteem and self-worth went to Hell. Working with John, I have discovered that this is very common for widowed people.

It hasn't been easy, but I am so proud of myself for rebuilding."

Today, Allison is enjoying life again, even through the pain that will always exist.

"I can play with my kids and I enjoy being their mother again.

When Austin died, the old me died with him, but I have done something that I never thought possible.

I rebuilt myself into a stronger and more loving woman.

I hope that he can see us, and I hope that he is proud."

Sometimes, the grieving want company.

And, sometimes, they want to be left alone.

The truth is, we almost always want the invite.

Where does everyone go?

Complicated Grief is a MF'er

"We were together for 18 years and had 6 children together. It was discovered that he had been molesting one of our daughters for a year. About a week after this truth came out, he completed suicide. My daughter is thriving, as she now works to help other children speak out when something like this is taking place. I am so proud of her, for being so strong and for using her pain for a greater good. That being said, the devastating situation still haunts us to this day. He was not the man that we thought he was. – Jennifer

"Do you know what it feels like to pray for your husband's death? I do. I would pray for him to die, because I couldn't take the abuse anymore. I couldn't take it anymore, so I would pray for it to end. When he died, I could leave. Finally, I was free. I used to feel guilty about praying for someone to die, but I don't feel guilty anymore. If he had lived, I would have been a prisoner for the rest of my days. I don't feel guilty anymore. Not even one bit." – Jill

"About a year after my husband took his own life, I actually smoked crack once. I wanted to experience it to see what was so great about the drug that he chose over me, over and over again. Logically, I know that he was addicted and could not stop, but to this day I still struggle with the emotional feeling that I was not good enough." – Christi

"No one prepares you for this, for complicated grief.

It is so odd loving him and hating him, all in one breath."

Jamie

Jayne

"He asked me when I was going to get over my dead husband. It was our first date. I was taken aback. I could not believe that those words came out of his mouth."

"What did you say?" I asked in response.

"I told him I would never get over my husband.

I then told him that I would be moving forward with my life.

But certainly not with him."

Jayne, one of my coaching clients, then proceeded to grab her coat and immediately left the date.

"How did it make you feel when you said that and left?" I asked.

"Amazing. And empowered," she responded.

Jayne is a badass.

#be #like #jayne

Dating Tip #734

if they are jealous of a dead person

they probably aren't a strong enough person

for you

Widowed people do not want sympathy.

We want:

Patience ~ even when you are tired of being patient.

Support ~ even when the rest of the world thinks we should no longer need support.

Understanding ~ even though we know it is impossible for you to truly understand.

Widowed people want to feel loved.

Welcomed.

And not forgotten.

Widowed people want to feel respected.

For the love that we had.

And for the love that we will always have.

For the loss that we have endured.

The pain beyond anything that we can properly articulate even with the most powerful of words.

Widowed people do not want to be seen with pity.

But instead.

View us as fighters.

Because we are.

Fighting so hard.

As tired as can be.

A helping hand is always welcome.

As opposed to a kick.

While we are already down.

Widowed people do not want to be viewed as scary.

Please don't worry.

We are not contagious. #promise

Widowed people want you to stick around.

Even after the dust settles.

And everyone goes back to their normal lives.

For it is us who is left with the pain.

The void.

And this new reality.

One in which we never asked for.

Widowed people want you to stop judging.

For you have no idea of what you speak.

Just as our love was unique.

So will be our grief.

And our eventual healing.

Widowed people want you to know.

That this pain we are fighting through.

Fuck.

It has taken its toll.

And that every time we think we can no longer go on.

Somehow we find the strength to rest.

And then rise.

The ability to grieve ~ as we move forward.

And to move forward ~ as we grieve.

Are both very real things.

Thus we ask that you please expand your mind before assuming that we are either stuck in our pain.

Or no longer in pain.

The inability for some in society to realize this somewhat simplistic concept leaves us even more hurt and exhausted than we already are.

Widowed people.

Surrounded by the ashes.

Of everything that we once knew.

The strength that it takes to hold on.

And then to eventually rebuild.

Honestly: **I'm so proud of you.**

the fourth eyelash on the right side of my left eye is killing me today.

i don't have a punch line here.

it just really hurts.

"I returned home about a week after my husband passed away.

After having a breakdown upon entering our bedroom,
I was finally able to compose myself and I decided I was going to try to take a hot bath.

As I went to run the hot water I noticed a pile of his finger and toe nails near the drain.

He must have cut them the morning of the day that he died.

As the tears reappeared, I scooped them up quickly with my hands, as though they were gold."

Stephanie

Rachel

"When my husband was alive, he never wanted to go to the store or do errands with me.

'Nope' would always be his go-to, even though he knew how much this annoyed me.

After he passed away, and was cremated, I kept a small amount of his ashes.

I wear him in a locket around my neck.

Now, whenever I have things to do, I always take his locket and ask him if he wants to go with.

I start off imitating him by saying, 'ra-ra-ra-ra.'

'Oh, you don't get to go awwww, that's too bad!
Now you have to go everywhere you never wanted to go,' I say with love.

Sometimes, when I am out, I will continue the conversation.

Especially now, since he no longer has the ability to talk back."

Sneak Peek of My Upcoming Book
My Michelle

When I stood up to speak the eulogy, I looked out and there were a lot of people. I had thought I wanted to honor Michelle in this way, but now I was just tired, just sad, just depleted.

My soul was crushed.

I didn't know if I would be able to get through the first word without crying, expecting myself to have a complete breakdown the likes of which I had so many times during her cancer battle.

Somehow, I made it through, speaking the words I had wrote quickly and worked to perfect over the course of a couple weeks, while I focused my mind on something else, something better and something magical.

Our wedding, the dream night we had thought about for so long that never did occur, stolen from us right along with our 50 years.

I spoke, people listened, but my mind was imagining that fairytale night when we would become one in front of all of our family and friends.

I imagined getting ready that morning—hopefully, I would look decent, maybe even semi-good. It was a rare occurrence, but sometimes I could actually look handsome on my absolute best of days. I imagined seeing everyone as they entered, friends and family coming up to me, one by one, as I'd already be fighting back the tears well before go time. I imagined the wedding procession and the beautiful songs we had picked. My mom and Joe first—I'd keep it together for them, I predicted—followed by all of the children. That is when the tears would begin. I imagined the twins, Michelle's toddler niece and nephew. They'd likely bumble and stumble a bit until finally making it to their appropriate destination. The room would be filled with smiles and laughter as each set of children walked down. I imagined the candles, the flowers, and the romance of it all. Hundreds of candles surrounding us as we would say our vows, purple rose pedals scattered throughout the beautiful room.

And then, I imagined the song starting to play.

No, not the traditional bridal song.

Michelle and I had picked "At Last" by Etta James, a song I had loved forever and that fit our story so perfectly.

Everyone would stand. I'd fight with all my mite to not completely lose it at this point.

And then, I imagined her.

Michelle.

Walking down the aisle we had created for her.

I imagined the dress she loved so dearly and how I would react, seeing her in it for the time.

I imagined the stunning shoes she picked out—yes, that third and final pair. I imagined the perfectly placed hair and makeup. She'd be more beautiful than ever before.

I had dreamt about this moment since I was 17 years old.

This moment, with this girl, the love of my life.

I imagined the tears I would shed, the beauty she would radiate, and the happiness we both would feel.

I imagined our vows.

I'd surely be crying at this point, rather hysterically. Her a single tear, maybe more. After all, she had been showing more emotion as of late, maybe there would be a second tear, or a third.

And then, I imagined the dance. Our first dance. We had picked the most romantic of songs, "Unchained Melody" by The Righteous Brothers.

Years of history would go into that dance, from a powerful and true teenage love, to years apart and an implausible reunion neither of us could have imagined in our wildest dreams.

From the first time we saw each other again to the romantic engagement over a decade in the making.

From an epic cancer battle, to the wedding of our dreams.

It was supposed to be our dance, our moment in time, the ending to a fairytale romance and the beginning of 50 years of happiness and joy.

I imagined this knowing it was a dream.

A dream that could no longer come true.

I read the words I had written for my beautiful wife, somehow managing to cry steadily throughout without completely falling apart.

I read and people listened.

I honored her, as she deserved to be honored.

i've been losing some weight lately and I just have to say.

my butt looks kind of cute in these sweatpants now.

#yes #i #looked #at #my #butt #in #the #mirror #in #order #to #make #this #assessment

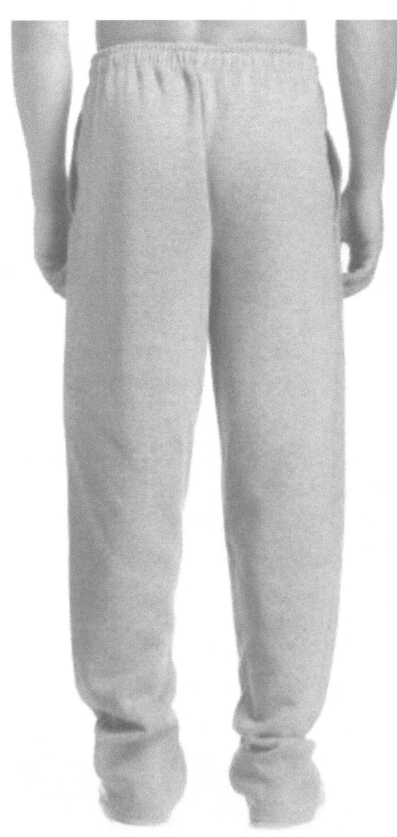

#there #is #something #wrong #with #me

#i #know

Meet Jerry

"WOW, that is the most beautiful man I have ever seen."

Those were the words written in a letter from Eric to Jerry,
as Eric recalled his thoughts on the night that the two would first meet.

August 18, 2007.

"We met at a party in Los Angeles, and although we did not tell each other that we loved each other for a few weeks after that, we both believed and knew it was love at first sight," Jerry said with a smile.

The two had finally found what they had been searching a lifetime for, each other.

"Eric took my missteps and mishaps of past relationships and smoothed them away and then, artfully, he filled my heart with his presence, his love, his care, his concern, and his support. He kept it just on the brink of overflowing, but always left room for more."

At the time of their new love, Jerry was 45 years old, and Eric was 40 years old.

"We meddled our lives while at the same time melting each other's hearts.
I stepped into his silliness and he stepped into my seriousness."

Just over eight years into their love, in October 2015, Eric was diagnosed with stage-4 cancer.

"There was no warning or indication that he might be sick.
We were shocked, as I know so many people are upon hearing those dreadful diagnosis words."

Thirteen months later, on November 23, 2016, Eric would pass away at 50 years old.

"Eric ran that path [of diagnosis and treatment] with such force, gratefulness, composure, compassion, and bravery that I have ever seen or known. How he was able to handle varied treatments, daily information, and discomfort, and still bring his 110-percent approach to us and every job and designer client truly stumbles my brain and words."

Jerry describes his other half as funny, sexy, warm, and always up for a
great chocolate dessert and a Sunday flea market adventure.

"Eric left such an imprint on my heart and my soul. On my everything. The truth is I want my love story back. We were so far from being done. We had so much more to share, and so much more to say.

Throughout the relationship, we would write love letters to each other often. I still write them to him today."

In an effort to still feel closer to Eric, Jerry occasionally wears
his love's favorite plaid shirts and his watches.

"John, I still wish. I still hope. I still wonder. I still love him. And I always will.

We never got the opportunity to finalize our wedding plans, as we always thought we had time.

With every hospital stay we had, varied staff would urge us to marry in the chapel.

All of the nurses became friends and fans, and would joyfully ask if they could be our flower girls and attendants!"

In memory, and in keeping with Eric's compassion and wish to give back, Jerry started a foundation to add custom benches to a special healing garden at the hospital to remember the staff, care, connection and love offered to the both of them during the many stays at St. John's.

"When I look back at the fact that we never got married, I am at peace with it.

We defined our love for each other each and every day in actions and words and with my family's love, so that was our commitment.

And, those love letters that we would write to each other – those were the only 'piece of paper' that we needed."

as i lay on the floor sobbing – and without the ability to stop – i calmed myself for a moment

it was in that moment that i could hear the birds chirping, the cars passing
and the children laughing as they waited for their school bus

the sun peaked through the curtains of the master bedroom that was now only mine

& no longer ours

that was when i first realized the harsh reality

the world does not stop for your pain

even when it feels as though the pain has stopped your world

July 26, 2012

I remember every detail of that night.

I cried as I read her the letter I had written.

The letter professing my love to her.

50 beautiful years awaited us.

As man and wife.

"We're getting married, John. I can't believe we're getting married."

That's my wife.

In her wedding dress.

A wedding dress that I never got to see her in.

We were married at the courthouse a few days before her first surgery was scheduled to take place.

We rushed there. To become man and wife.

Not knowing if she would make it out of the surgery alive.

After the cancer came back and she was terminal, we decided to plan a real wedding.

She didn't make it to that real wedding.

She died two weeks before it was scheduled to take place.

I have so many regrets.

Not getting to see her walk down the aisle is atop that list.

But, she got that dress. Her dream dress.

She loved that dress SO much.

While at hospice, she would talk to people about how great the wedding was going to be.

She wasn't coherent enough to realize that she wasn't going to make it there.

Michelle died without me ever seeing her in that dream dress.

A week after she passed away, I stumbled across this picture in her phone.

I lay motionless in bed, both happy and devastated.

Tears flowing down my cheeks as I laughed aloud at the memory of how giddy it made her.

My bride.

In her dress.

I want to live a long life.

I want to remarry and have grandkids.

I want to write and teach.

I want to spread my message to the world.

I want to tell them everything I have learned about love, loss, grief and healing.

But.

When it is my time, I am running up there.

No – I am sprinting up there!

To see her.

For so many of us, we didn't just lose our spouse.

They were also our best friend.

And our person.

The truth is ~ **no longer having your person** ~ may just be the loneliest feeling of all.

Meet Alma

*"I saw a picture of the most handsome man I had ever laid eyes on.
His green eyes captivated me. I was not able to look away."*

It was on a fall day in September of 2012 in which Alma was taken aback by the man who would become her future husband, as she suddenly stumbled upon his picture on social media.

"I can recall being in fourth grade and all the other little girls asked me what my 'Prince Charming looked like.' I would always say that he would have green eyes and jet black hair. Little did I know back then that I would be describing Grant, the man I would marry."

At the time, Grant was enlisted in the Marine Corps and stationed in Camp Lejeune.

"We began talking and it was just so natural. We felt like we had known each other for years."

A month later, the two would finally meet in person when Grant was able to come home for the Thanksgiving holiday.

"When I saw him in person, he was even more beautiful than I had imagined. I could not believe that I was so lucky to have a man like him be interested in me," Alma recalled.

"From 2012 to 2016, we had a long-distance relationship, and he was deployed overseas twice during that time. We were given many hurdles, but our relationship always came out stronger."

In November of 2014, Grant asked Alma to be his wife and the two exchanged vows on January 1st of the next year.

Six months later, Grant would say goodbye to the Marine Corps as he finally had the opportunity to go home to the woman that he loved.

"We were so excited to end the distance and start our new life together. I had been in a relationship with this man for almost five years and still he gave me butterflies."

Just under one year later, on April 11, 2017, Alma got the phone call.

"I could not believe the words I was hearing. The love of my life was gone. My whole world stopped. Our plans, our future, our everything, it was suddenly taken away from us."

Grant was 26 years old at the time of his passing. Alma was just 23.

"A week before he died, he sent me a text message.

It said, 'I love you the moistest, even more than your most.'

"I miss his beautiful, green eyes and his cute smile. I miss his wit. He could be blunt and snarky, but he was so funny that I could never stay mad at him.

Most of all, I miss the way that he loved me.

He was my protector, even if he did like to be the little spoon as we cuddled."

Mark

My wife, Lynn, passed away at the age of 43.

At the time my step-daughter was 19 and about to return back to college.

Her biological father is still alive.

"You are legally an adult. We haven't discussed this yet but you are free to choose where you want to call your home," I said to her.

"Mom and I had talked about that a couple of years ago, and I couldn't see myself staying here with you, but now that I have to choose, I can't see myself being anywhere else," she responded.

I love that child as my own, *because she is*.

I was on a first date a couple of weeks ago and the woman I was with said she didn't want dessert but I ordered some for myself anyway because I love dessert and then I offered her some and not only did she eat more than half of it but she took the last bite without offering it to me and I would have been fine with that but she didn't even ask if I wanted it how do you go from not wanting dessert AT ALL to HOGGING the entire dessert I don't know but needless to say there will NOT be a second date because homie don't play that and if you're wondering why this is the longest run on sentence in the history of the world and how someone who always writes in fragments can produce a sentence such as this one it is because that cheesecake was AMAZING and I am still VERY unhappy with this ENTIRE situation.

They Say

"Ronnie and I started dating in high school. About four years into our relationship, he ended it with me. My heart was shattered. Six weeks later, he came back to me and wanted to get back together and, although I was curious as to why he broke up with me in the first place, I never asked. For 47 years we loved each other, but as much as I hate to admit it, our past always bothered me. I always wondered about that short six-week break and why he would do such a thing. I know that when it is my time, Ronnie will be waiting for me with open arms, and when that time comes, I'll be ready to do something that I wasn't fully able to do while he was here. I will be ready to embrace my future with him, without a concern of the past." – Penny

"Somewhere in the back of my mind, I knew that my husband was a big deal in our community, and not just for being married to my wonderful self either. The magnitude of his impact didn't really hit me until after he died, though. We knew Bytheal was a coach, but I don't think we realized that in our town, he was also a legend. Sometimes you just want to escape your grief, even if only for a moment but, with all the lives that he touched, it seems as though every time I leave the house I am reminded of the love that the community had for him. As amazing as that is, it can also be a hard thing to deal with. Sometimes it feels as though the wound is being reopened. When all I really want to do is let it rest." – Lisa

"Once Ed got my attention and I realized that he was sending signs to me, he began to go a little overboard. To the point where I had to ask a medium to tell him to please scale it back a little. He was such a jokester when he was alive, I'm not surprised he is still like that now" - Dawne

"The stillness echoes louder and louder
in the emptiness.

Voices and laughter from days gone by
haunt the now empty spaces in our heart.

You find yourself yearning
for what was lost.

Pleading for one more kiss or
"I love you,"
but it doesn't come.

Only the silence."

Kim

421 Days a Widower

FOR THE LOVE OF APPLE CIDAR VINEGAR
if one more person asks me how I can still be in love with Michelle,
but be ready to date, I am going to lose my mind.

I will always love Michelle.

But, I want to find something special again.

#you #have #no #depth

"Sometimes, anger is the only feeling I have.

I'm used to anger.

I understand anger.

I can deal with anger.

I can't deal with the fact that my husband is dead.

It is too painful, so I go to anger.

I need it so that I can feel something.

I need to feel something, so I know that I am not dead, too."

Cristy

sometimes anger is simply sadness

with no place to go

Krystal

"For me, one of the hardest parts of losing Chad,
other than having to live without him, has been the guilt.

For so long, the guilt of not being the perfect wife stood in my way of true healing.

Once, during a coaching session, I remember John asking me if I thought I deserved to be happy.

It was in that moment that I realized I did not.

It hasn't been easy but, slowly, I am beginning to turn the corner.

I am beginning to realize that I deserve to be happy, and that I am once again worthy of love."

if you don't think that you deserve to be happy

we need to work on that

They Say

"After Garry passed away, I would go to the grave and literally lay down on top of it for hours at a time so that I could be close to him. I can't imagine how that looked to any passersby that saw me but, at the time, I didn't care." – Anita

"Michael and I were married for 47 years. For 47 years, it was him and I. When he died it, all of a sudden just became 'I.' I was convinced that my life was over. Even if I was still breathing, I was convinced that I would never actually live again. It took a while, but I have rediscovered my smile. John once told me that the goal was to 'walk forward, even with the pain'. I thought that he was crazy at the time but, now, I see that such a thing is possible and that is exactly what I have chosen to do." – Linda

"Honestly, after 42 years of marriage, I only think about Judy when I'm breathing." – Michael

Dear Hope,

I am finding you again. You're in my kids' smiles as they run and play.

You're in the laughter I don't fight to suppress anymore.

You're in the summer plans that we're making for park dates, the splash pad, or our garden.

You're in seeing and feeling hearts open again to take a chance not knowing what will happen but still yearning to try.

I didn't know that you'd come back.

You snuck in when I wasn't looking and have stayed when I tried to push you back out.

I've missed feeling hopeful and I know there is so much still to come.

Love, Jenny

The people that you choose to surround yourself with post loss are going to have a monumental impact on your grief.

And your healing.

#choose #wisely

cry with someone you love

over someone you love

the hurt will be real

and the healing profound

This is How You Show Support

"My husband's best friend came up to me the day of the services and told me that Carl had made a promise. A promise to love me for the rest of his life. Her words were so comforting, because I realized that she was right, and that he had done just that." – Stephanie

"My friend moved into my house for a month. She slept in the bed with me, put water and food in front of me and was there for support every moment of every day. Looking back at that time I honestly don't know what I would have done without her. Thank you Michele."- Linda

"A couple of weeks after he passed away a bunch of family came to visit. I remember I went to the beach to just sit there, I had to get away from all of the noise. As I sat there I felt someone come sit next to me, and grab my hand. It was my aunt Lucy. She just sat there, holding my hand in silence. That moment meant everything to me." – Lisa

This is NOT

*"I told my always-so-judgmental friend that I missed having sex with my husband
and she told me that such a comment was inappropriate.
I responded by telling her that her face was inappropriate and then I walked away.
In hindsight, perhaps I could have dealt with the situation better, but how dare she." – Jessica*

*"A family member said that my son, who was 12 when he lost his dad,
was using his anxiety as a crutch. My daughter was 5 when Dylan passed.
It amazes me that a grown adult could say such a thing about a grieving child
who is struggling to learn a new normal, one without their dad." – Candice*

*"Three months after my husband passed away suddenly, my mom stood across from me,
with her hands on her hips, and told me to suck it up and move on.
Mind you, at this point she had been happily married to my wonderful father for 42 years." – Becky*

*"What support? Everyone scattered.
Like a bunch of cock-a-roaches." – Steph*

Meet Ashley

And her precious daughter.

Natalie Mae.

Ashley gave birth to her beautiful little girl on February 2, 2017.

"The day she was born, the epidural failed so I wasn't numb for the C-section.

The pain was beyond intense, but the only thing that took it away was hearing my daughter cry for a couple of seconds, right before they took her out of the room."

Natalie was born 9 pounds and 14 ounces.

She was 21.5 inches long.

"She was born completely blue. She was airlifted to the University of Iowa Stead Family Children's Hospital where they were finally able to intubate her and get everything under control.

They weren't able to transfer me due to my blood pressure being too high.

I finally saw my daughter for the first time on February 5th."

You see, at the twenty-week ultrasound, Natalie was diagnosed with a heart defect.

"I was told she would be able to live a long, normal and healthy life," Ashley recalled.

After her birth, complications continued to arise, and Natalie had her first heart surgery on February 9, 2017.

Just seven days after being born.

"She was in the hospital for the first month of her life.

I remember being terrified when they told us we were ready to go home.

The thought of not having professionals around to help me if something were to go wrong was extremely overwhelming."

After going home, Natalie continued to battle.

Doctors' appointments were followed by trips to the emergency room, and long hospital stays.

Every day Ashley wondered if her little girl would make it through.

"Finally, after about seven months, it was time for her big surgery. This would be the second time they would be stopping my baby's heart as they would keep her alive with a machine."

Natalie's surgery lasted almost twelve hours.

"Twelve hours of waiting, of waiting to know if my daughter would be okay.

When they came out to tell me that everything went well and that she was okay, the relief I felt was beyond words. It was over. The worst of it was over."

Ashley had been told that her daughter wouldn't need another surgery for five years.

"It was finally time to start focusing on what a mother should get to focus on with her baby:

Teaching her the best words (mama!), tummy time, crawling, walking, playing, and laughing."

It was their time now.

Their time to rid themselves of doctors, and hospitals, and surgeries.

Their time to enjoy the bond that they had created.

"She learned to say 'mama' and we tried different baby food," Ashley recalled.

Peach and apple oatmeal were her favorites.

Along with vanilla custard pudding.

"She was getting to the point where she could sit up on her own.

She even learned to fake cry.

It was hilarious," Ashley joked.

Natalie Mae loved giving hugs and kisses, and she loved to head-butt her mom.

"Holding hands was a necessity in order for her to fall asleep at night, and her favorite thing in the world was to make me laugh."

Not only mother and daughter, the two were also best friends.

Things finally seemed normal.

"We would spend hours and hours during our days just laughing back and forth at each other."

On October 27, 2017, after complications with Natalie's breathing, Ashley called the paramedics and rushed her daughter to the emergency room.

"I rode in the front of the ambulance. When we got to the hospital, I got out and started walking towards the doors, following them while they carried her."

Once there, they took Ashley into a different room.

"I remember it being small and empty."

After an hour, the doctor entered the room.

"She looked at me, and she shook her head.

That moment.

That moment is what still takes my breath away."

Natalie Mae had passed away.

Just short of nine months old.

Her time was limited.

But her impact, well, that was beyond measure.

"Before I got pregnant, I was in a very dark place.

Natalie showed me a love and a light that I never knew existed.

She showed me my purpose.

The truth is, John — *Natalie saved my life.*

The way that she looked at me.

She was my biggest fan.

It is because of her, *that I realize I am worthy of love."*

I'm like 97 percent sure I just swallowed a fly.

I'm really not sure what to do right now.

But I'm scared.

#im #really #scared

The Evolution of a White Boy

22-year-old John:

"I will never date a widow," I responded to my mom.

"Why not?" my sister asked me in a taken-aback tone.

"Hell no. I'm not going to compete with a dead man."

32-year-old John:

"I don't care if the love I have for my wife makes all potential new love interests run away.

Any woman who doesn't understand a heart large enough for two, lacks the depth that I require."

That's growth.

i miss Michelle yelling at me for all of the many things that I would do wrong

such as breathing oxygen

and peeing while I stand up

I will never forget the people who sat with me.

As I was broken.

I will never forget the moments.

In which they were there.

Thank You

When You Washed Her Back

The nurses and hospice staff kept asking me if I wanted them to give Michelle a bath.

I said "no" the first few times. I didn't want to disturb her.

I was scared.

Every time she would get up, she would suffer from God-awful hallucinations.

She was finally resting comfortably and I didn't want to take any chances.

"How do you feel about us giving her a bath today, John?" they asked again—for the third day in a row.

After asking a handful of questions to ensure that she would not wake up, or be disturbed, I reluctantly agreed.

As they prepared to give my wife her sponge bath, I was equally scared, and nervous.

She was teetering on sixty pounds at this point. So fragile. So close to the end.

They told me they were about to begin, so I went and sat on the couch in her room, just about ten feet from the hospice bed which had now become her home.

In walked Kim, Michelle's friend.

"They're about to give her a bath," I said. Frazzled.

"Oh," she said back.

I gently shook my head, as to show her my concern.

As I looked over, I could see one of the nurses removing Michelle's shirt, while the other nurse closed the curtain.

Her back.

I saw her back.

The back that I use to massage.

The back that I use to kiss.

"You have the sexiest back," I would tell her often.

"You're so weird, John. It's a back!" she would say back with a chuckle.

"No, it's your back," I would respond, awestruck that such a beauty would even look at me twice—
let alone be my wife.

That back.

Her back.

The one that I loved.

That wasn't the back I saw on that cold, white January day.

What I saw was something that scared me, and scarred me.

Something that is still embedded into my brain today, just over seventeen months later.

A back so thin, so brittle, and so worn that a husband could not help
but be forever damaged from the sight.

"Would you mind if I helped them, John?" Kim asked.

"Bathe her?" I responded back, surprised.

"Yes," she responded.

"No, not at all."

To others, it might seem like a simple act of kindness.

A routine gesture from a friend wanting to help care for a beautiful soul
who was nearing the end of her human experience.

But, to me, it was so much more.

To me, it was an act of love that would provide a comfort to Michelle, when I could not do it.

To me, it was one of my wife's favorite people caring for her, in a moment in which I was incapable.

To me, it was—and is—a memory that stays with me to this today.

So heartfelt and genuine, that it balances out the horror of an otherwise unbearable moment.

eventually, I realized something

any person who made my life MORE difficult when my wife was sick ~ or after she died ~

no longer needed to be

a part of my life

if they have already shown you that they don't understand

at some point you are going to have to understand

that they'll never understand

I made a list of funny memories that Michelle and I shared.

I look at it often.

It is one of the many tools that I have created for myself to help along the way.

I would encourage you do to the same.

The funny memories that we shared…

This is my friend, Malia.

Her husband, Nathan, passed away.

Malia was so determined to take her girls to the daddy/daughter dance that she posed as a man.

Today ~ Malia is my hero.

Don't Forget Our Children

Don't forget our children.

As the days pass by.

Don't forget our children.

Those that had a daddy or a mommy die.

Don't forget our children.

As you go on with your day to day routine.

Don't forget our children.

Truly profound loss, they have seen.

Don't forget our children.

They deserve better than to wonder where everyone went.

Don't forget our children.

Love and support for them is so critical, when received, it sometimes feels Heaven-sent.

Don't forget our children.

Just because they wear a smile.

Don't forget our children.

If you think they are "just fine," you may be the one who is in denial.

Don't forget our children.

The pain is forever there.

Don't forget our children.

The little girl who quietly wishes her mommy could help her with her hair.

Don't forget our children.

The small boy who wishes his dad was around to help him with his favorite sport.

Don't forget our children.

They don't deserve to feel intense pain of this sort.

Don't forget our children.

Just because you don't see the tears.

Don't forget our children.

You can't imagine our profoundly deep, inner fears.

Don't forget our children.

The ones who cry out at night.

Don't forget our children.

"I miss my mom."

Such a cruel and heartbreaking sight.

Don't forget our children.

"Why did daddy have to die?"

Try explaining to a young child why they had to say goodbye.

Don't forget our children.

It hurts them and thus it hurts us, too.

Don't forget our children.

They need us, but they could really benefit from you.

Don't forget our children.

Moments and days in which they feel that haunting pain.

Don't forget our children.

With your love and presence, they could truly gain.

Don't forget our children.

Muffins with Mom and Donuts with Dad.

Don't forget our children.

Each new occasion brings with it a special type of sad.

Don't forget our children.

Mother's Day and Father's Day, too.

Don't forget our children.

The absence of those we lost, if you only knew.

Don't forget our children.

At a young age, they had a parent die.

Don't forget our children.

Their souls cry.

Don't forget our children.

The reality is, though, that even if you do, it will be okay.

We'll put on our capes.

And be their lone heroes.

Again today.

When we cry in front of our children.

We give them the unspoken "okay" to cry.

When we hurt in front of our children.

We give them the unspoken "okay" to hurt.

When we grieve in front of our children.

We give them the unspoken "okay" to grieve.

This is a gift.

Sometimes, when I type my name out at the end of an e-mail, my fingers miss the "L" in my last name.

They miss the "L"

Thankfully, I catch it before I press "send."

#but #it #is #always #a #close #call

Do you know how many kids get bullied at school because they have a dead parent?

Too many.

Although, in fairness, one kid getting bullied at school for having a dead parent is too many.

I see it often on Facebook, and elsewhere.

A parent posting that they are in bed with their child.

Who is sobbing.

Uncontrollably.

Because some kid at school mocked them for having a dead parent.

PSA:

If you are raising a child who would do this, you are raising a little asshole.

You better do something to turn that around.

Right now.

Whatever you are doing at home.

It. Is. Not. Working.

It's not.

Fuckin.

Working.

This type of thing is disgusting.

And vile.

These children already have to grow up without a parent.

Because they are dead.

The depths of such pain.

Is both agonizing.

And profound.

To have to deal with this shit on top of it.

Is beyond words.

Talk to your kids.

Teach them about bullying.

About what is right.

And about what is wrong.

Teach them how to be respectable humans.

Who don't spew words of hurt.

And hate.

For fuck's sake.

This is not okay.

it feels like yesterday

and, yet, it also feels

like a lifetime ago

those happy moments

in which the sadness is there

that is the scar on your heart

speaking out

Nice Guys Don't' Always Finish Last

Garry and Kim met in an AOL chat room in the year 2000.

"I remember on our first date, I opened the car doors for her as well as the doors to the restaurant we went to. She thought it was so strange, and I thought it was strange that she thought it was strange," Garry recalled.

After their first date, Garry and Kim would see each other for two more dates before it happened.

"After our third date, she told me that she couldn't see me anymore, but she didn't tell me why. Finally, a few days later, she told me the reason."

Kim told Garry that he was too nice.

"I got really pissed. We were on the phone when she said this and I kind of went off. I ended up hanging up on her and I went to the batting cages to let off some steam."

A few days later, the two would talk and Kim would ask to see Garry.

"On what would now be our fourth date, Kim told me that she thought maybe I was a psycho because I appeared to be too nice. She then told me that her friend told her that she was the crazy one for letting me go.

She told me that she was glad she saw my backbone when I got mad and hung up on her."

Seven years after their first date, with his kindness and backbone both firm in place, Garry and Kim would become man and wife.

He was 36 and she was 31.

The two had their entire future ahead of them.

"Kim was the kindest, most caring individual. She was so great with kids and she loved everyone, and everyone loved her.

We had such a great marriage."

Sixteen years into their love, Kim would pass away suddenly from a pulmonary embolism that occurred as an after-effect of an ankle surgery that she needed due to a freak car accident.

She was just 40 years old.

"I was in shock for quite some time before the reality hit. Being a widower is so lonely and overwhelming. I miss her more than anything. She was not only my wife but she was my best friend, my lover, and my life.

She was my everything.

Sometimes, I think back to our first date and to how she found it so strange that I opened all of the doors for her.

I hope that when it's my time, I will see her first.

And with a big smile on her face, this time, she will be holding the door open for me."

incase you're wondering:

1. grief brain is a very real thing

2. you're not the only one who hates the grocery store now

3. sitting in the car doing absolutely nothing because you don't want to go in the house is quite normal

4. i had a peanut butter and jelly sandwich for dinner tonight

5. and losing your spouse really fuckin sucks

grape jelly is alright

#but #strawberry #is #my #fave

Her death has created a depth to me.

To my mind. To my heart.

And to my soul.

I no longer see the world as I once did.

The truth is ~ while I absolutely hate how I got here.

I appreciate this depth.

I value this depth.

I now struggle to relate to those.

Who may not share this depth.

At some point, you are going to have to grieve.

Your way.

At some point, you are going to have to live.

Your way.

At some point, you are going to have to stop giving a **SHIT**.

What other people think.

Healed

I hate the word "healed."

I'm sorry.

I just do.

I fractured my elbow when I was about 12.

I was trying to be cool on my bike and I flipped off of it.

Do you know what happened to my elbow eventually?

It healed.

It no longer hurts.

....

For the rest of my days, I will love Michelle.

For the rest of my days, I will miss Michelle.

For the rest of my days ~ in one form or another ~ I will grieve Michelle.

....

I have and will continue to find healing.

Absolutely.

Healing is possible.

And, at some point, necessary.

But I will NEVER be FULLY HEALED from the loss of my wife.

#get #out #of #here #with #that #shit

grief changes

and it evolves

absolutely

but ~ no ~ it never actually ends

not after a truly profound loss

                        i will love my spouse, miss my spouse and grieve my spouse for the rest of my days

                                            &yet I will also smile, laugh, love and live

                                                      as i carry this every-changing pain

We ARE ALL SO WEIRD!

"After Daniel passed, I placed some of his ashes in my lingerie drawer. I know that if he couldn't be here with us, that drawer is definitely the place he would choose to rest." – Christine

"I still have the pants that Dave was wearing when he went into hospital for the last time. A friend found them when we were tidying up after the funeral. After a few minutes, he asked if I was okay and I said I could still smell him on them. He then gently pointed out I was sniffing the crotch area." – Lesley

"I wore my husband, Tim's, boxers to my first gynecologist appointment after his death. I figured that was the closest I could ever get to having sex with him again." – Terri

Last week, I was talking with one of my coaching clients.

She was expressing her disappointment with how she will never again experience the youthful bliss of young love.

A love filled with hope and excitement.

A love not marred by the devastation of all that has occurred.

....

I agreed.

....

But.

....

While that particular beauty may never be felt again, I think that other loves can be just as beautiful.

....

One in which two broken souls find each other along this rocky road that we call "life".

....

And together, they realize something.

....

The broken.

....

Are beautiful.

....

Too.

My wife had an extremely difficult life.

To put it mildly.

And in the most simplistic of terms.

But you would have never known it.

Ever.

She was warm.

She was kind.

She was SO funny ~ without even trying to be.

She would light up every room she would walk into.

I would often look at her.

Amazed that she was the way that she was.

After having been through so many of the things that she had endured.

I will never be the person that she was.

Never.

I am not capable of it.

But I try to use her as an example of the person that I want to be.

One moment in particular really stands out to me.

We were on our way home from seeing the cancer specialist in NYC.

We had just received even more devastating news.

The fears that we wanted to rid ourselves of ~ but had held onto for so long ~ were becoming more and more set in stone.

She was going to die.

As we entered the line at the airport, I took exception with what I perceived to be an attitude from the TSA agent.

The old John wanted to, and was about to, say something.

"Stop it," Michelle started.

"He is not responsible for our pain."

I remember shutting my mouth in anger.

Anger at the TSA agent.

Anger at the world for doing this to us.

And yes ~ anger at her.

For being right.

I will never be the person that my wife was.

Never.

No matter how hard I may try.

But as I continue to grow as a man ~ and more importantly as a human ~ I strive to remember how she was.

How warm she was.

How kind she was.

How her presence would instantly make others feel better.

I try to remember that the world is not responsible for my pain.

I try to not allow the ugliness of some humans to turn me ugly.

I try to lift people up.

Having seen the impact such a thing can have on another human.

The ability to ~ make or break ~ another living person.

Is an actual thing.

And most importantly.

I try to do what she did.

I try so hard.

To not allow an often ugly word.

To turn me cold.

after hell

peace

becomes your #1 priority

Listen to me:

You can rebuild.

Yes, you can.

Meet Guadalupe

I had known Salomon in high school, but we never did communicate much at all.

He was the popular jock, and I was the somewhat nerdy academic.

A few years after graduation, I attended a party, and he was there.

Sparks flew.

As if the only time we had was the moment, our love grew quickly.

We moved in together within a few months of dating, as his words of admiration toward me and his belief in my goals were that ocean breeze to the skin, and summer warmth to my soul.

I got pregnant shortly after, but we ended up losing the baby. I was devastated.

Salomon loved me through it all.

"Why are you still here? I have so many problems that aren't yours, nor from you," I remember asking him often.

"Because you are worth it. It won't always be like this. And you are worth it."

One lazy Sunday afternoon as we laid in bed, tears rolled down my cheeks, along with a smile.

He asked me what was wrong.

"I've never loved someone like this. I can feel this in my soul."

"I feel it, too," he responded as he failed to fight back tears of his own.

After a lifetime of knowing what I wanted out of this life, I finally had it.

"Do you want a back massage, babe?" he would ask me the night before his passing.

I had gotten pregnant again, and the expected pains were beginning to take their toll.

That night, after a wonderful back massage and a kiss goodnight, I awoke at 3:00 a.m. from a nightmare.

I had dreamt that Salomon was no longer here and that I would have to raise our baby alone.

Woken up from my sobbing, Salomon turned around and asked me what was wrong.

"I just don't ever want to do this without you."

He gripped my hand, and said the last words that he would ever say to me:

"It's okay, baby. Everything will be okay. "

The next day, at the age of just 25, the love of my life would pass away suddenly in a motorcycle accident.

My life and everything that I knew evaporated, in a moment.

I found myself a young widow without a clue of what to do or how to survive.

On June 5th of that same year, just three months after the passing of the father he would never get to meet in the physical form, I gave birth to our son.

Tito.

....

One evening, as Tito was approaching eighteen months old, we sat in my car in a nearly-empty parking lot, eating fifty-cent Jack in the Box tacos.

With tears falling down my face silently, as to not scare him, I thought about how this had become my life.

I was a widow, I was a mom and, now, my son and I were homeless.

Sleeping in my car for the night, I woke up the next morning knowing that this was not something that I could

do long-term, so Tito and I would go from house to house of both family and friends.

I would purposely change it up so that nobody would notice we lacked a roof over our head.

Calling homeless shelter after homeless shelter in a sea of desperation, I was constantly denied.

All of them, always full.

....

"Thank tú, mamí," Tito said as he jumped on the fresh, white sheets, hugging his doggy pillow as he laughed from the belly.

I looked at him and was inclined to ask him what he was laughing at, and what he was thanking me for.

But I didn't because, the truth is, I already knew.

Taking in the moment and the beauty of our new home, I asked him for a hug and, with the biggest smile you can imagine on a child, he widely opened his arms and held me tight.

Although Salomon was not with us during that moment physically, I could feel his love shining through."

The other day I got my lip stuck in between the tiny gap that I have between my two front teeth.

For 25 minutes.

I was FREAKING OUT.

And hyperventilating.

I could not get it out.

This is my life now.

#this #is #my #life #now

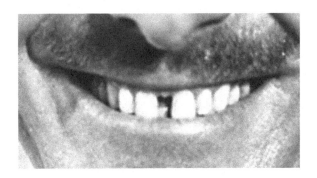

"I was somebody's someone.

Then, one day, in a horrible, cruel, and sudden twist of fate, my somebody was gone.

When you are somebody's someone, you are tethered to them.

When they go away, that tether is cut, severed, sliced.

So you drift, desperately trying to reattach to your somebody but to no avail.

You drift further and further away from your somebody.

When your somebody goes away, you are no longer their someone, and you begin to feel like you are no one.

This is the part of widowhood that nobody warns you about."

Sharyn

"Sometimes, I look at my life and all that I have been through, and I wonder if it was real.

I wonder if it's real now.

I have known the depths of such agony over and over again.

I have been so close to giving up.

To be honest, this newfound happiness scares me,
as sometimes it feels as though I am waiting for the other shoe to drop.

I find myself in a constant fear that it will all just go away.

That, once again, I will lose everything that I love."

Lee

grief is so predictable

and yet

grief is even more unpredictable

About eighteen months after Michelle passed away, I sat at the bereavement group that I occasionally went to and I told the others there that I didn't really cry anymore.

I wasn't saying it to brag; it was simply a statement of fact.

For the last few weeks, at least, the tears had stopped.

One week later, I had the absolute worst day of all the days since Michelle had passed away.

I sobbed openly, and without the ability to stop, for eight consecutive hours.

The tears were so powerful that my insides physically ached and I thought my eyeballs were going to pop out of my head.

moral of the story:

grief, does indeed, come in waves

I feel cheated.

We were robbed of our 50 years together.

I feel lucky.

I got to call the love of my life "my wife."

I feel cheated and I feel lucky.

I feel both.

"And that's the thing about watching someone you love die of cancer, or another terminal illness.

At first, you're crying out to God – or whoever – for them to be saved.

And then, after watching them suffer for so long, you find yourself crying out for them to be taken.

Their suffering becomes so intense that you find yourself begging for them to be released from their pain.

For the vision before you, you can no longer take."

Me

"Is it okay if I come, John?" Arieona asked.

"You can come, but she's in a coma-like state so she's not going to wake up. Just want you to know," I responded.

It was around midnight.

A few days before Michelle passed away.

I was tired.

And lonely.

I was devastated.

And depleted.

After waiting awhile, Arieona finally arrived.

I greeted her at the front door of the hospice facility, which had become like a second home.

"She won't wake up. But they say if you talk to her, she can hear you," I informed Arieona as I took my seat in the lounger next to Michelle's bed.

As the woman who was once like a sister to Michelle gently climbed into the bed, the tears began to flow.

For her.

And yes.

For me.

It had been nearly a decade since they had seen each other.

Arieona began to gently caress Michelle's face.

I cringed.

I always cringed whenever anyone would touch her.

She was finally comfortable and I didn't want her to be disturbed or woken.

"It's you. You're here," Michelle said as she slowly came to.

It had been days since she awoke or spoke.

"I'm here."

They hugged so tight.

"I've missed you so much," Michelle said.

"I missed you, too," Arieona responded.

"Are you coming to the wedding? You have to come. My dress is so beautiful. I look like a princess in it," Michelle proclaimed.

Looking at me through the tears, I knew that Arieona's glare in my direction was a request for direction.

I nodded gently as I wiped the falling tears off of my ever-thinning face.

"I'm coming, Michelle. I wouldn't miss it for the world."

Dear widowed people,

If you've fallen for someone after your spouse passed,
only to come to the realization that they weren't the right one.

And you let them go.

Bravo.

Because, honestly – that shit right there.

Is brave.

And you WILL be okay.

The first heartbreak after your loss can be devastating.

It can make you feel as though you are back at square one.

There are actual reasons why this is the case.

Please know that you are not foolish for the way that you feel.

For the pain that you feel.

I felt it, too.

Honestly the self-sabotage that I see every day is really sad.

I am thankful to those who allow me to work with them to try to stop this type of behavior.

Some of y'all literally ruin any – and every – chance you have at happiness, because you either lack self-worth.

Or are overflowing with fear and guilt.

At some point, you have to try to fix this.

Or continue to deal with the consequences of being your own worst enemy.

Self-worth is everything.

Watching someone discover, or rediscover it - is a beautiful thing.

And self-sabotage has the ability to destroy your life.

Watching someone avoid that – let me tell you – it's everything.

"I couldn't see myself enough to help myself."

Erin Miley

"I was once that man. When the thought of hope did nothing but fill me with rage."

Me

The writing, coaching and speaking are no longer just a hobby.

They are my passion. And my profession.

I know that deep despair.

I know that feeling of no hope.

When you're on the floor crying so hard that your insides hurt.

& you are left gasping for air.

I know that feeling of being stuck.

The vision for a better tomorrow ~ simply does not exist.

I know it.

I have felt it.

& I have lived it.

But I also know that it is possible to survive.

To exist.

& then ~ eventually ~ to live again.

I know it.

Because it has happened to me.

& for so many others.

I know that feeling.

That feeling of hopelessness.

That feeling of worthlessness.

It's that feeling of:

"Why am I even going to try anything, when nothing is going to help?"

I get it.

I was there.

But, now, I am here.

It is my mission in life to help the broken.

The abused.

Those that struggle with self-esteem.

& self-worth.

Those that are guilt-ridden.

& grief-stricken.

Those who continue to self-sabotage their life.

Over and over again.

It is now my mission in life to lift people up.

To show them hope.

& to help them rebuild.

I am, and always have been, a talentless fool.

Until now.

Until this.

So, if you're ready to take this journey with me.

If you're ready to work through the fear.

To honor the pain.

And to pursue a better tomorrow.

Let's do this together.

Areas of Focus:

- Love and Loss
- Grief and Healing
- Abuse and Toxic Relationships
- Self-Esteem and Self-Worth
- Dating
- Self-Sabotage
- Parenting
- Life Purpose, Motivation and Goal Setting

#coach

i know this piece is in my first book

but y'all loved it so much

i had to put it in this one, too…

STFU

Sit Down. And Shut Up.

Sit down.

And shut up.

Serious question: Is your spouse six feet under?

Oh, wait, are they a pile of ashes?

No?

They aren't?

Wow.

Okay.

Cool.

Then sit down.

And shut up.

My wife's name was Michelle. She's gone.

Once a widow. Always a widow.

Once a widower. Always a widower.

Sit down.

And shut up.

Unless you watched your spouse die.

Unless you buried your spouse.

Unless you burned your spouse.

Sit down.

And shut up.

Do not tell a widow or widower how they should be living.

Do not tell a widow or widower how they should be acting.

And, please – for the love of all that is right in this world, PLEASE – do NOT tell a widow or widower when they should try to love again.

I am sick of seeing widows and widowers vilified for trying to pick up the pieces of their lives.

I am sick of seeing widows and widowers vilified for trying to find companionship again.

For trying to find love again.

Hell, for trying to find ANYTHING again!

We are lost souls. On a journey to find our self again.

And YOU want to judge?

You?

Do you know the courage it takes to go back out there after your spouse has died?

After you watched them die of cancer. Or a massive heart attack. Or suicide.

After you watched them fall to 60 pounds. Having bowel movements on themselves. Having horrific hallucinations so bad that seeing them like that strangled your soul.

After you watched them fall to their knees. And clutch their chest. And take their last breath.

After you walked in on their body. Dead. Because they took their own life.

You have no idea.

Do you have any idea how badly the loss of a spouse messes with your mind?
With your heart? With your soul?

No. You don't.

So sit down.

And shut up.

You are not allowed to judge.

You are not allowed to pass judgment as you drive home to your spouse.

You are not allowed to pass judgment as you eat dinner with your spouse.

You are not allowed to pass judgment as you cuddle up on the couch with your spouse.

You are not allowed to pass judgment as you have sexy time with your spouse.

You. Are. Not. Allowed. To. Pass. Judgment.

Sit down.

And shut up.

Stop judging.

Stop thinking that you know what the Hell you are talking about.

Because you do not.

Your life wasn't ripped from you.

Your future wasn't destroyed.

Sit down.

And shut up.

This was not our choice.

This was not a breakup. Stop comparing.

This was not a divorce. Stop comparing.

This was not the loss of a grandpa. Stop comparing.

This was not the loss of Uncle Thomas. Stop comparing.

And, for Heaven's sake, this was NOT the loss of your damn CAT. Stop comparing!

This was the loss of a soulmate.

Our love.

Our other half.

Our life.

Our future.

Sit down.

And shut up.

The next time you see a widow or widower try to pick themselves up, dust themselves off and "get back out there."

You have 2 choices.

You can either sit down and shut up.

Or:

You can give them a standing ovation.

For their heart. For their courage. For their bravery.

Those are your two options.

And your ONLY two options.

Because. You. Do. Not. Know.

Rant. Over.

Mic drop

Ever since Michelle passed, I no longer match my socks.

Like.

EVER.

Ain't nobody got time for that nonsense.

#bad #boy #for #life

The Walk

I had to leave that day.

I had no choice.

Rarely did I have to leave Michelle's side.

And when I did.

It would kill me.

But I had to leave that day.

I had no choice.

Michelle was still in the hospital, recovering from her first major surgery.

The final walk-through of the house that we had started to build
just a few months before she got sick was scheduled for that day.

I had to leave.

I had no choice.

"Are you okay?" I asked seconds after the final walk-through wrapped up.

"Yes, just tired, I'm going to try to go to sleep," she responded on the other end of the landline phone.

It had been weeks since I left the somehow now-
comfortable confines of the hospital in which we stayed.

Normally, I would have rushed back.

Eagerly maneuvering through traffic in order to get back to her side as quick as possible.

But, that day.

That day was different.

It was a beautiful August day and I needed to breathe.

I needed to take in the fresh air.

And clear my mind a bit.

Even as the thought of doing so brought with it a tremendous amount of guilt – since she could not do the same.

I walked.

With no end sight – and no direction of where I was allowing my legs to take me – I walked.

I just walked.

I walked and I thought of all we had been through.

In our youth.

The years apart.

The reunion.

And the illness that so cruelly threatened to destroy our future.

I walked.

And I thought.

I thought about what we were days away from achieving.

The purchase of our dream home.

The start of what should have been the beginning of 50 beautiful years together.

Finally, somehow – someway – the walk ended.

My mind more scared.

Yet, clear.

My mind more confused.

Yet, hopeful.

A sea of contradiction to be sure.

But such is the case with cancer.

And love & loss.

Or, in this case, the threat of loss.

The threat of losing your everything.

As I got back into my 2004 Saturn Ion, a song came on.

That song.

"Fight Song" by Rachel Platten.

A sobbing fool.

I would become.

I returned back to the hospital and held Michelle's hand.

She smiled.

Her having no idea the emotions of my day.

And me having no idea the emotions of hers.

Today.

I went for a walk.

A walk along that same very path that I walked that beautiful August day.

Just over five years ago.

A walk along that same very path that I have walked over and over again.

Both with her.

And since her.

This walk was different, though.

This walk was the day before our final goodbyes.

The day before our final goodbyes to the house that we built.

To the house that became a home.

To the home that housed so many of our dreams.

And our fears.

Moments of clarity on this walk.

Interrupted by memories of a life together.

A life cut short.

The happy times.

The horrible times.

The end times.

And everything in between.

With each step, I felt a deep sense of sadness.

Only to be combated with.

A more profound sense of hope.

The Last Words I Heard

*"The ironic thing is, we never said 'goodbye' to each other. Ever. Except for that day.
As JohnE left that morning for work, he stopped, he kissed my forehead,
and he whispered, 'Goodbye, beautiful.'
Little did we know that the first time we would say 'goodbye'
would also be the last time we would say 'goodbye.'" – Constance*

*"A couple of days before he died I was changing Eric's colostomy bag.
With his eyes closed he whispered 'I'm so embarrassed'.
I assured him that he didn't need to feel that way. He just wanted it to be over already,
and as much as it broke my heart, I can't say that I blame him.
I just wanted him to know that I would do anything for him, since he always took care of me."
– Lorraine*

*"My husband passed away of a heart attack, on top of me, during an intimate moment.
His last words to me were, 'Let me just catch my breath.'
It has been a long journey to get here, but I finally feel as though I am catching my breath.
I feel as though I owe that to him. Since he was never able to catch his." – Wendi*

Anne

"Traci had been unconscious for a couple of days and no one could explain to me why she was getting worse again.

It was ten days before she passed away.

I was leaning over the bed and stroking her hair,
and it was at that moment that she slowly opened her eyes.

I was right near her face, my right hand holding her left.

We just looked in each other's eyes for a long, silent moment.

'How did I get so lucky?' I asked.

'No, I'm lucky,' she whispered back.

I told her again that I was lucky, and that I loved her so much.

'I love you more.'

Those four words would be the last four words that I would ever hear from my wife.

Traci may no longer be here, but our love and that moment live on."

Meet Aisha

I thought so hard about what to post today.

The truth is, I put a tremendous amount of thought into every word that I write on this page.

Then, last night, at about 8:00 p.m. – it hit me.

Aisha.

I forgot to write about Aisha.

A few months ago, I asked those who follow this page to share a picture of someone they loved and lost.

The response was overwhelming.

Over the course of the days that followed,
I spent hours looking at all of the photos of those who were loved and lost.

My heart felt both happy and heavy.

Happy that so much love was shared.

Heavy that so much loss had been endured.

Then, I saw Aisha.

Aisha took my breath away.

Aisha loved fairies and rainbows.

She loved unicorns and dolphins.

She was a foodie.

And her favorite color was purple. #so #is #mine

Aisha's parents, Nirosha and Gopi, describe her as "the most sparkling little girl you could ever meet."

I never had a chance to meet Aisha but, based on the smile
I see in the photographs that she shines in, I might have to agree.

Aisha was diagnosed with cancer in 2015.

She passed away on November 24, 2016.

She was 6 years old.

Aisha leaves behind her mom, dad, and older sister, Amaya.

On that day, a few months ago, Aisha took my breath away.

After seeing her picture, I was so touched that I asked Aisha's mom if she would ever be interested
in allowing me to share her daughter's smile with a larger audience.

She said that she would.

I filed the e-mail away and told her that I would be back in touch with her when the time was right.

At 8:00 p.m., on Thanksgiving Eve, as I sat and considered what to post on Turkey Thursday, it hit me.

Aisha.

I forgot to write about Aisha.

"I asked her to send me a sign today, and then you e-mailed me,"
her mom said moments after I hit the "send" button.

"My fear is the world forgetting her, but today is showing me that she will never be forgotten,"
she concluded.

Aisha loved playing with slime and Shopkins.

Aisha, and her breathtaking smile, will never be forgotten.

They died.

But the love doesn't have to.

Instead of being ashamed of what you have been through.

Be proud of what you have survived.

& overcome.

Battered, bruised and maybe even broken.

But still, somehow – you rise.

I am proud of myself because…

"I survived...

now, I want to live."

Rikki

March 18, 2019

I woke up so profoundly sad today.

The longing for my wife hits hardest in the mornings.

The ability to roll over and see the love of my life beside me ~ is no longer there.

Reaching for my phone, I picked it up to see that I had missed
an early Monday morning call from my doctor.

Test results.

For sixteen long years I have felt this way.

Like shit.

The knowing that something was wrong with me only grew more and more frustrating
as a result of being told.

There was nothing wrong with me.

As I opened up my computer, I saw the two words I was expecting: Multiple Sclerosis.

To be honest, I had known for quite some time that this is probably what it was.

A lesion here and a lesion there ~
walking hand in hand with so many of the symptoms of this particular chronic illness.

But, an official diagnosis always evaded me.

Upon reading the results, most people would have felt helpless, upset, or demoralized.

All of those feelings may soon come.

Believe me, I know that.

But, for the moment, I actually feel validated.

Empowered.

And, most importantly ~ I feel determined.

Determined to do what it is that I need to do to get better.

Determined to get better so that I can lead the life that I actually want to lead.

I have come too far.

And fought too hard for those that I love.

To now give up.

On myself.

Eleven years to the day that we buried my dad.

I feel as though a shot of life has been injected into my soul.

Fuck this. And fuck that.

I have too many dreams to give up now.

The dreams of a career in which I help millions, instead of just thousands.

The dreams of falling in love again one day, the empty side of the bed no longer leaving a permanent ache on my soul.

The dreams of being able to have more dreams and more dreams.

The dreams of living a life.

That I actually want to live.

I have always fought for everyone else.

Now it's time that I fight for me.

I am going to kick this thing's ass.

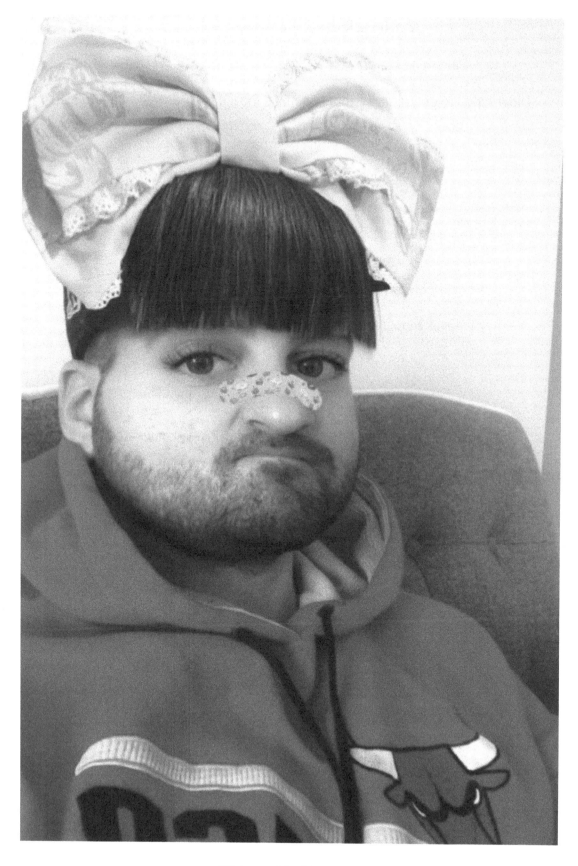

snapchat 4 life

there is nothing more beautiful than witnessing laughter

from a once-broken soul

"I am the me that doesn't know me anymore, that doesn't know the person that was born from this tearing away."

Zoe

"I was Doll before I ever met Bruno.

I am still Doll.

It took me 2 1/2 years to come the realization that

I am more than my husband's widow."

Doll

"I'm so sorry I couldn't save you Michelle,"
*I wept to her as we laid in the hospital bed together,
a few days before she was to be transferred to hospice.*

"You did save me John. Now I need you to save yourself," *she responded.*

"The hardest part of this horrible journey has been having to go from 'we' back to just 'me.'"

Ashley

"My husband took his life.

I refuse to let him take mine."

Charmaine

Dear Jessica, You Are Not Alone

Up until this very moment, I have only admitted this to a few close friends but, the truth is,
I occasionally get frustrated with my work.

I pour so much of my heart and soul into it, exposing my deepest thoughts and emotions.

I get frustrated because I feel like I have such a story to tell, such a journey to share –
and, yet, my platform isn't big enough.

I want to grab a bullhorn and shout it from the top of a tower.

Everything I have learned about love, loss, grief, healing, and that undying hope for a better tomorrow.

Something funny happens every time I feel that way, though.

Just as I begin to question whether or not to continue on this path,
I receive a message, a comment, or an e-mail from someone.

Someone telling me what my words have meant to them.

Someone telling me how much our story has touched them.

And how thankful they are to have found my voice.

When that happens, I am reminded of something that my wife told me while she was dying.

As I wept over her like a baby, telling her how much I hated this world, a world in which such a
beautiful soul could develop such a rare and aggressive cancer at such a young age.

"Well, we cannot change the world. Bad things will continue to happen.
But, if you can use this pain to help one person, for them the world will be forever changed.
So, make something good come out of this," she said.

Those words have stayed with me to this day, as have so many of the words she said to me.

A brave soul that, even while dying, comforted her husband an equal amount
of times as he comforted her.

I feel that there is something bigger on the horizon for me.

A larger platform to tell our story and help others.

I can't quite put my finger on it, and I'm not entirely sure what my next step should be.

The combination spoken above causing a further frustration and lack of patience.

Sitting at the airport, waiting to board my plane to fly back home from a weekend trip, I received an e-mail from Jessica.

It reminded me of something so important.

That message that Michelle so gracefully delivered to me.

The size of the platform does not matter.

Instead, it is the size of the message being delivered that counts.

Dear Jessica,

I receive so many messages from people that touch me deeply, as did yours.

In fact, your message made me tear up.

Perhaps it was the travel fatigue, or the fact that I am on a four-hour flight home suffering from a stomach bug that sent me into crybaby mode – but I think it was more than that.

I think it was the line about your husband's eyes.

The line you wrote about how the pain in his eyes watching you near death is worse than the pain you are feeling.

I know that pain.

I have lived that pain.

Those words brought me back to a place I don't often visit, but that is forever burned into my memory bank – just below the surface of where I allow my mind to travel on a regular basis.

It brought me back to watching Michelle die.

It was so long.

And it was so painful.

Two-and-a-half years of pure hell.

It brought me back to the moments in which I couldn't control my raw emotion, and I would break down in front of her.

A grown man so destroyed that I occasionally failed at providing my wife with the support that she needed, and deserved.

But, then, you said something else.

You told me that my words simultaneously broke and mended your heart, at least a hundred times.

And, selfishly, I felt a sense of peace.

Peace that I could do something that helped a stranger now realize that she is not alone in this journey.

Peace that you now know your husband's pain has been felt by many before, and will be felt by many after.

Peace that you know that, tragically, he is not alone.

I can tell you that my heart has broken and mended more times than
I can even begin to count, or remember.

The expected outcome of losing the love of your life for the second time, this time ~ for the rest of time.

After you told me about your story and how my writing has touched you,
you finished the e-mail with a series of questions.

So, let me answer those for you right now.

"How is it to actually lose a spouse?" you asked.

It is awful.

It is so far beyond awful.

It is painful and gut-wrenching.

It is heart-breaking and soul-crushing.

It is all-consuming and life altering.

It is as if someone has taken a knife to your insides and will not stop stabbing them,
without conscience or guilt.

**"Was it all worth it, meaning, would you do it all again even knowing
that Michelle was going to die?"** you asked.

Yes, Jessica ~ it was all worth it.

All of it.

Every single second.

Of every single day.

Hope, the only thing in this world that can combat fear.

The love shared, the only thing stronger than the heartbreak endured.

"Do you think my husband can make it if I don't?" you concluded.

Yes.

Your husband can make it.

And, I believe your husband WILL make it.

I believe this for one reason: I made it.

When people hear me say that I was as low as a human being could go when Michelle was dying, they often wonder what I mean by that.

I believe that my words are self-explanatory.

If the worst happens to you.

The pain will be unbearable for him.

There will be moments when surviving the next minute seems impossible, let alone the next hour ~ or day.

Moments in which the shattered soul left on this Earth to grieve the departed
will want nothing more than for God to call their number in hopes that the pain will go away
and that the beautiful reunion will take place.

I know.

I was there.

But, now, I am here.

Still grieving my wife

Still loving with my wife.

Still with a heart that does not quite tick the way that it once did.

Still with a soul that will never quite be one hundred percent repaired.

But, I am here.

Because I survived.

Because I existed.

And because somehow, someway:

Now I Live.

Should this happen, should you be forced to go - tell your husband that he is not alone.

Tell him that others have felt his pain.

And that others know his heartbreak.

Most importantly, tell him this:

Tell him that love does not end in death.

Tell him that the reunion will take place.

Tell him that it will be more beautiful than he could have ever imagined.

Until then, tell him to grieve. And to grieve hard.

Tell him to live. And to live with purpose.

Tell him to reach for happiness, laughter, and most importantly ~ peace.

Tell him to carry the love that he has for you with him.

Each and every day.

Tell him, Jessica, *that you'll only be a thought away.*

Thank you for reading my book.

I hope you found it helpful, humorous and healing.

As an independent author, word of mouth is everything.

And the truth is, people cannot read a book that will help them, if they don't know that the book exists.

If you believe this book will help others, please consider recommending it on Facebook, Instagram, Twitter, etc.

I love you peoples.

Sincerely,

John Poo

www.betternotbitterwidower.com